D0929821

SMOKING

SMOKING

SMOKING

HERBERT TAREYTON
CIGARETTES
Cork Tip
TRADE MARK
CROSS-CUT
CIGARETTES
MANUFACTURED ONLY BY
W. DUKE SONS & CO
DURHAM, N.C
USA
DUKE'S
CAMEO
CIGARETTES
THESE CIGARETTES ARE MANUFACTURED
ON THE BONSACK CIGARETTE MACHINE
ORIGINAL
TRADE
PIN HEAD
MARK
CIGARETTES
LA FLOR DE
ANNA HELD
MODERN
MODERN SIZE

SMOKING

BY SHERRY SONNETT

A FIRST BOOK

FRANKLIN WATTS | NEW YORK | LONDON | 1977

Cover design by Frances Jetter

Illustrations courtesy of: American Brands, Inc.: frontispiece, 9; Rothco Original/Serrano: facing p. 1, Bernhardt: p. 24, Punch: p. 54; The New York Public Library Picture Collection: pp. 4, 14, 16, 18, 19; Ohio Historical Society: p. 8; Rare Book Division, The New York Public Library, Astor, Lenox, and Tilden Foundations: p. 12; Grolier Picture Library: pp. 27 (Nellie D. Millard and Barry G. King, authors, W. B. Saunders Company, publisher of "Human Anatomy and Physiology"), 32, 35, 45; American Cancer Society: p. 28; American Lung Association: pp. 37, 51, 56; American Heart Association: pp. 41, 43; United Press International: p. 58.

Library of Congress Cataloging in Publication Data

Sonnett, Sherry.

Smoking.

(A First book)
Includes index.
SUMMARY: Presents the history of smoking and how it affects the body.
1. Tobacco—Physiological effect—Juvenile literature. 2. Smoking—Juvenile literature. [1. Smoking] I. Title.
QP981.T6S65 615'.782 77-5419
ISBN 0-531-01299-9

Printed in the United States of America
5 4 3 2 1

CONTENTS

SMOKING

SMOKING

SMOKING

"I know it's not good for me but
I just can't stop smoking!"

When you stop and think about it, tobacco smoking is a very strange habit. Imagine a visitor from another planet landing on Earth. All around, the visitor would see people setting fire to the leaves of some plant, breathing in the smoke, and blowing clouds of it out of their noses and mouths. If you picture the scene in this way, smoking begins to seem a little odd.

The link between smoking and disease has been proven beyond a doubt. Even so, people have smoked for hundreds of years and will continue to do so. Why *do* people go on smoking even though they know it is an unhealthy and dangerous habit?

There may be no clear answer. But an investigation has to begin somewhere, so the first question is, how did smoking begin?

TOBACCO AND THE INDIANS

Tobacco is a plant that at first grew wild all over the North and South American continents. There were over sixty varieties. The main types were *Nicotiana rustica,* which grew in the north, and *Nicotiana tabacum,* which grew in the south and became the parent of modern commercial tobaccos. Tobacco is a member of the nightshade family and some kinds have large, handsome flowers. The common petunia is a distant relative and gets its name from *petum,* the Tupi Indian name for tobacco.

The plant is very adaptable and can grow in a wide variety of climates, from tropical jungles to temperate plains to arid mountains. Some types have large leaves, others quite small ones, and each plant puts out pods with thousands and thousands of seeds. Every known variety of tobacco was originally found in the Americas. Tobacco smoking is one of the few customs that can be called strictly American in origin.

THE MAYANS BEGIN IT ALL

Nobody knows how the first person got the idea to burn tobacco and inhale the smoke, but historians agree that that person was a Mayan Indian. The Mayans had a great civilization that was at its height when Jesus Christ was alive. It covered what is now southern Mexico and Central America. Mayan civilization declined, for reasons that are still shrouded in mystery. But they left behind great temples and pyramids and passed many of their customs onto their successors, the Toltecs and the Aztecs. One of their customs, tobacco smoking, spread to almost every other Indian tribe throughout North and South America.

A Mayan carving is the earliest representation of tobacco smoking. It was found on the Mayan temple at Palenque in southern Mexico and shows an old man in a fancy headdress blowing smoke through a long, straight pipe. The man is a *shaman,* or medicine man, and he is probably offering the smoke to the gods as a prayer for rain. It is likely that at first tobacco was always used as part of a religious ritual or ceremony. It is not hard to understand why. The strong Indian tobaccos could produce strange states of consciousness in the smoker. The smoke itself, as it hid things and drifted up to the heavens, may have looked magical and mysterious.

MAYAN BELIEFS ABOUT TOBACCO

The Mayans thought tobacco smoke could keep away evil winds and poisonous snakes. They believed it could protect night travelers and those who worked in dark places. They also believed that shooting stars were burning cigar butts thrown away by the *Balam,* or Jaguar Rain Gods. These gods ruled over the four corners of the universe. In one of their ceremonies, they blew tobacco smoke in the four directions to appease the gods.

In one ceremony, called "The Interrogation of the Chiefs," a series of riddles was asked. One of them was: "Son, bring me the firefly of the night. Its smell shall pass to the north and to the west. Bring me the beckoning tongue of the jaguar." What does the Chief want? The answer to the riddle is a smoking tube, or cigarette, of tobacco. The firefly is the cigarette, and the jaguar's tongue is a light.

Cihuacoatl, the powerful Goddess of the Earth, had a body filled with tobacco. Mixcoatl, the God of Hunting, was generally pictured with a gourd containing tobacco as part of his costume. The Mayans also believed tobacco and its smoke could cure illness, protect an unborn child, and rid a dwelling of ghosts and evil spirits.

OTHER INDIAN BELIEFS ABOUT TOBACCO

Almost every tribe that smoked tobacco had religious or magical beliefs about it. The Caribs of Brazil blew smoke over their warriors to give them courage in battle. The Indians of Virginia cast powdered tobacco on stormy waters to appease the gods and improve their fishing catch. The Osages always smoked before doing anything important and invited the Great Spirit to "come down; smoke with me as a friend."

This temple carving from Palenque, Mexico shows a medicine man blowing smoke as part of a religious ritual.

The Karuks had a myth about a Winged-One, called Savage-One-of-the-Middle-of-the-World. He frightens the Sun, called He-Who-Travels-Above-Us, with tobacco smoke until the Sun promises to protect him in time of war. Another Indian tale is about Long-billed Dowitcher who loses his five children to Mountain Man. He finally kills Mountain Man with stones. Then he puts his children's bones in a lake and brings them back to life by smoking and blowing the smoke over them.

Like the Mayans, other tribes believed in the power of tobacco and its smoke to calm angry gods, give courage, cure illness, bring rain in time of drought, or turn back the waters in time of flood. The Indians thought tobacco could do just about everything—if you used it right.

SMOKING BECOMES AN EVERYDAY AFFAIR

Because tobacco was so plentiful and easy to use, Indians began smoking tobacco outside of religious ceremonies. By the time Columbus landed, they had already developed all the ways of smoking that would soon spread around the world.

The Mayans used long clay pipes in their rituals, but they preferred cigarettes for their personal use. These were very much like modern cigarettes except that they had no paper. Instead they wrapped the shredded tobacco in corn husks, palm leaves, or some other material. They also smoked cigars that were made just like cigars are today. Sometimes they simply tied some tobacco leaves with string and lit up.

Some tribes preferred pipes to cigarettes and cigars. Archeologists have found beautiful examples of pipes in both North and South America. They were often decorated with animal symbols of power such as the eagle, bear, turtle, or frog. The Mound Builders of the American Midwest have left behind very elaborate pipes made of stone, clay, and wood, and some with hammered copper bowls. They rival the clay pipes the English would later perfect.

The Caribs even took snuff, which is powdered tobacco taken through the nose. They used a forked instrument, shaped like a Y, made out of bone or cane. They put the two ends in each nostril, the other into the tobacco and just sniffed. Although nobody knows exactly where the word "tobacco" comes from, some people think it was the Indian name for this instrument, which the Spanish misunderstood to mean the plant itself.

It seemed very odd to the Europeans when they discovered tobacco and all the ways it could be used—as cigarettes, cigars, pipes, snuff, even chewing. Imagine how startled the English explorer probably felt, in 1605, at being offered a lobster claw filled with tobacco to smoke! But it wasn't long before the Europeans tried the stuff, liked it, and brought it home to Europe.

Left: this clay pipe from the Adena Mound in Ohio shows a man with an elaborate headdress and earrings. Right: the Caribs sniffed tobacco through a Y-shaped tube.

TOBACCO CONQUERS THE WORLD

When Christopher Columbus sighted land on October 12, 1492, he was expecting to find the gold and riches of the East Indies and the Orient. Instead, he and his crew found people unlike any Europeans had ever seen before, people with strange customs and costumes. Because they still thought they were in the East Indies, the Spaniards called these people Indians. Columbus and his men did not find the gold they were looking for on the first islands they explored in the Caribbean, although gold would soon be discovered in other parts of the New World. But they found something else that was to become almost as valuable.

In his journal on October 15, 1492, Columbus wrote:

We met a man in a canoe going from Santa Maria to Fernandina; he had with him a piece of bread which the natives make, as big as one's fist, a calabash of water . . . and some dried leaves which are in high value among them, for a quantity of it was brought to me at San Salvador.

A few days later a landing party Columbus had sent ashore returned to report that the natives "drank the smoke" of those curious dried leaves. This was astonishing to the Europeans who had never seen anything like smoking before. For a long time they were puzzled and disgusted by this strange habit. They had no way of knowing that soon they too would be drinking smoke from those leaves, and spreading the plant and the habit of smoking it all over the known world.

THE SPANISH TAKE TO TOBACCO

By the early 1500s Bishop Las Casas, one of the first Europeans to write about the New World, wrote:

I knew Spaniards on this island of Española (Santo Domingo) who were accustomed to take tobacco, and being reprimanded for it, by telling them it was a vice, they replied that they were unable to cease using it.

From this and other writings of the period, it seems clear that the first non-Indian smokers were common

F
E
K
G
H
I
D
C
B
A

sailors and soldiers. They sampled tobacco, got hooked, and refused to give it up even though their officers and the clergy thought it was wrong. In fact, they began smoking in such large numbers that by 1535 the Spaniards decided to cultivate the plant. They established their first tobacco plantation on Santo Domingo, so that they wouldn't have to rely on the tobacco that was growing wild. Tobacco cultivation proved to be very profitable. They soon had other plantations in Trinidad and Cuba, in Mexico, and parts of South America. By 1575, they even had plantations in the Philippine Islands in the Pacific and had a complete monopoly of the world's tobacco trade.

THE PORTUGUESE LIKE IT, TOO

The Spaniards' closest rivals in tobacco use and trade were the Portuguese who, according to early records, began to smoke in Brazil around 1555. The Portuguese were excellent sailors and explorers, and they soon had trading posts down the west coast of Africa, the Indian peninsula, the Malay islands, and even China and Ja-

This sixteenth-century engraving shows tobacco being grown in an American Indian village, Secota (North Carolina). See the fields marked "E" in the upper left center, and lower left side.

pan. Wherever they went, they carried tobacco with them and introduced it to the different people they met. These people also quickly took to tobacco, and in this way the smoking habit spread across the world.

THE REST OF EUROPE FOLLOWS

During this time, other European countries were discovering tobacco and learning to smoke it. The Dutch, French, and English were all experimenting with growing tobacco in their colonies in the New World. But the tobacco grown in these colonies was not nearly as good as the tobacco grown by the Spanish. So other Europeans continued to buy from the Spanish the tobacco they actually smoked.

From the time Europeans discovered tobacco they had brought back samples of the plant itself to their home countries. Many private and royal gardens in Spain and Portugal grew various types of the plant. In 1559, Jean Nicot, the French ambassador to Portugal, sent some cuttings of the plant to friends in France. (It is from Nicot that tobacco gets its botanical name, *Nicotiana*.)

When Nicot returned to France, he convinced the Queen, Catherine de Médici, to use tobacco as a medi-

A seventeenth-century London "tabagie" (smoking tavern) where pipes were passed around from smoker to smoker.

cine in the form of snuff. He claimed he had cured ringworm, ulcers, and cancer as well as the wound of one of his cooks who had cut off "almost all his Thombe . . . with a great Kitchen Knife." The Queen was impressed and the use of snuff became popular throughout the French court. For centuries, taking snuff remained the only way for a person of "quality" to take tobacco. Ordinary people could smoke pipes or cigarettes. Aristocrats took snuff.

THE ENGLISH

It is thought that smoking became popular in England when students who had learned the habit at the University of Leyden in Holland brought it home. For young English dandies, smoking became a high art. They even hired "Professors" to teach them the proper way to fill a pipe, roll a cigarette, and even blow smoke rings! But you didn't have to be a dandy to smoke. Soon people from every level of society and all occupations were doing it.

The English didn't like having to buy tobacco from the Spanish. For years their colony in Virginia tried to grow a tobacco as good as the Spanish variety. They had no luck until (perhaps through the efforts of a friendly sea captain) the Virginians managed to get

This seventeenth-century print shows a group of elegantly dressed women smoking.

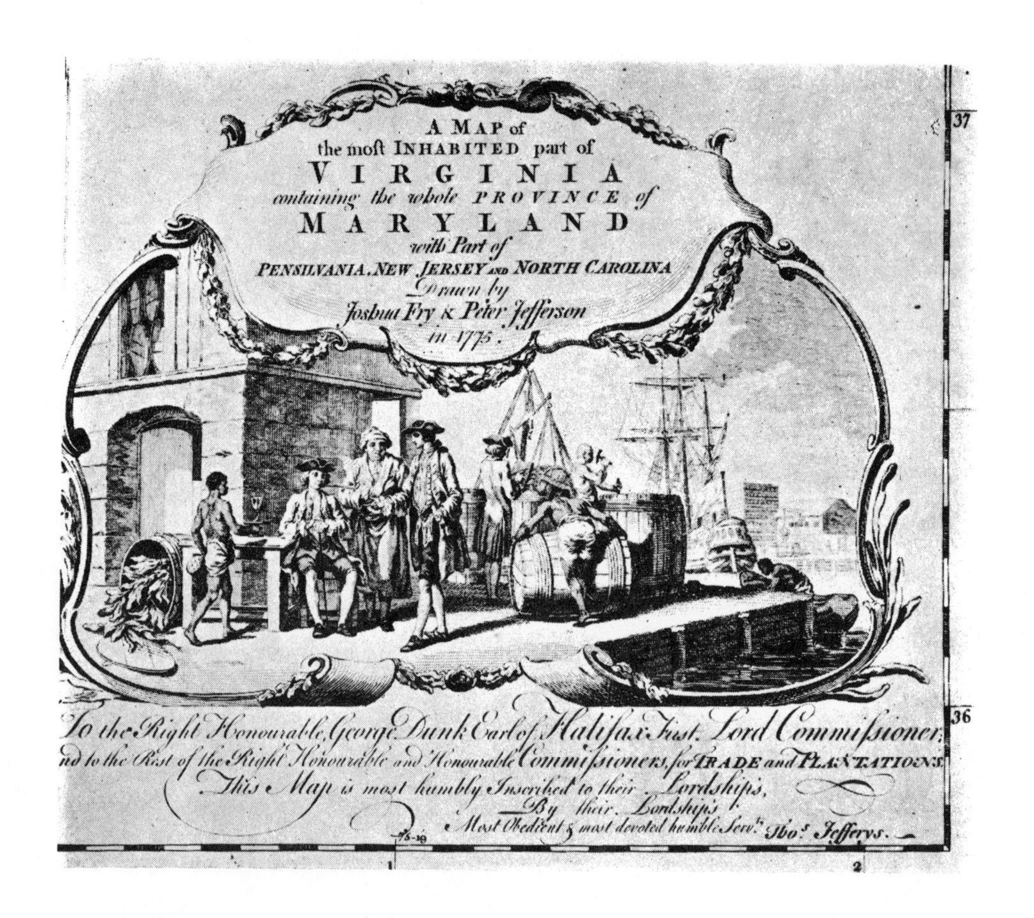

(Left) A familiar scene in the tobacco colonies included large barrels of tobacco leaf about to be shipped abroad. (Right) A sixteenth-century tobacco "factory" in the colonies. Leaves were twisted into a rope and wound tightly on a wheel. The rope could then be chewed, sliced into a pipe, or ground into snuff.

some Spanish tobacco seeds. By 1617, there was a tobacco boom in Virginia with every available bit of land being used to grow it, even the streets! It was the end of the Spanish monopoly and the beginning of the most important cash crop the English colonies had. Tobacco was so important in these colonies that it was for a time *legal tender.* This meant it could be used as money to pay taxes, debts, and even ministers' salaries.

TOBACCO AS MEDICINE

From the very beginning some people, such as the clergy, were against the use of tobacco. But there was another group which approved of it—the medical profession. Doctors and scientists all over Europe, and especially in France, were convinced that tobacco was the "magic" drug they were looking for. They claimed tobacco in all its forms—the smoke, the dried leaves, the liquid that could be extracted from it—could cure almost anything. Their list included colds, fevers, blisters and blemishes, coughs, even broken limbs. During the Great Plague epidemic in England in 1664–66, doctors advised schoolchildren at Eton to smoke a pipe each morning to keep from catching the plague.

This belief in tobacco as a medicine outweighed any objections church or state officials had. But most ordinary people didn't care either way. They used tobacco simply because they wanted to. And by the end of the 1700s, most of the medical claims for tobacco were proven false.

By the beginning of the twentieth century, tobacco had spread to every corner of the world. The English might prefer a pipe, the French snuff, or the Turks and Russians cigarettes. But all of them had been conquered by the least likely of things—a simple vegetable product.

SMOKING AND YOUR HEALTH

It wasn't until the 1920s that modern doctors and scientists began to investigate the effects of smoking on our general health. One reason it took so long is that before that time medical science just didn't know how to research the question. But another reason is that by the 1920s, larger numbers of people were smoking than ever before. The Industrial Revolution had brought machines to every area of manufacturing, and tobacco products were no exception. Machines could turn out millions of cigarettes in less time than it had taken people to make thousands by hand. And those little cigarettes, by themselves or in packs, were easy to carry around.

Now the tobacco growers and cigarette manufacturers (usually the same people) had to find the best way to sell their cigarettes. They turned to advertising, which was also a new business, and spent a great deal of money on ads that made smoking seem attractive and glamorous. Smoking began to look "grown-up," to be the "in" thing. More people began to smoke. Even women took up the habit in large numbers. And not only did more people smoke, but they smoked more.

For years, doctors and scientists pursued the question of smoking and health and kept finding connections between various diseases and smoking. But there were many people who would not believe that smoking was really dangerous. Lately however, especially since the 1964 U.S. Surgeon General's Report, which officially recognized the dangers of smoking, nobody has really questioned the harm that tobacco smoking does to your health.

SOME GENERAL FACTS

Countless medical studies have been done on smoking and health. We now know that, in addition to such serious and often deadly diseases as cancer and heart disease (which will be discussed in later chapters), people who smoke are in poorer health in general than people who don't smoke. For instance, smokers stay home from work because of sickness 45 percent more than non-smokers and have more colds, coughs, and the like. Smokers who have operations more often develop complications afterwards, such as pneumonia, than non-

"I wish somebody would catch us.
I can't take much more of this."

smokers. Male cigarette smokers get more stomach ulcers than nonsmokers, and they take longer to heal.

There's more. Smokers have a higher rate of gum disease and often get trench mouth, an ulcerlike condition of the gums that causes bleeding, pain, and bad breath. *Stomatitis nicotina* is a precancerous (not yet cancerous) condition of the mouth's palate caused mainly by pipe smoking. It clears up as soon as smoking is stopped. We also know that smokers have a weaker sense of smell because smoke destroys the inner lining of the nose.

But even more important are the facts about smoking and death. There is definite evidence that people who smoke die on the average at younger ages than nonsmokers. For instance, a man of twenty-five who smokes two packs of cigarettes a day can expect to live 8.3 years *less* than a twenty-five-year-old who doesn't smoke. Think about that. Eight years is an awfully long time. Doctors also estimate that for men between the ages of thirty-five and fifty-nine, one out of three deaths are "excess" deaths. That is, they could have been prevented if those men hadn't smoked.

It makes you wonder that, having all these facts and figures, some people smoke anyway. But tobacco has a special ingredient that keeps people coming back for more. That ingredient is nicotine.

NICOTINE

Nicotine is a poisonous substance. In its liquid state nicotine is oily and colorless. If a dose of sixty milligrams were swallowed by the average person, he or she would probably die. Taken in large enough doses nicotine can make you feel "high." The early tobaccos smoked by the Indians probably had very high nicotine contents, which would explain the accounts of trances and stupors reported by the Spanish.

It is possible that nicotine may be addictive. This would help explain why people have a hard time quitting smoking once they've started. According to this theory, it is the body's need for nicotine that can make a smoker light the next cigarette. But if a smoker does without nicotine for several days, his or her body chemistry changes and no longer feels the need for a "fix." Regardless of whether the nicotine is responsible, there is no doubt that smoking becomes a habit very quickly for most people.

The main effect nicotine has in your body is on your arteries. The arteries carry blood to every part of your body. (The veins carry it back to your heart.) Nicotine constricts the arteries, making them narrower. This makes it harder for blood to reach all the parts of the body where it is needed. To make up for this, your heart has to work harder to pump more blood through the arteries so that your body can get the oxygen and nourishment it needs.

TAR

Tar is another major ingredient of tobacco smoke. It is pretty much what its name suggests—a sticky, gummy

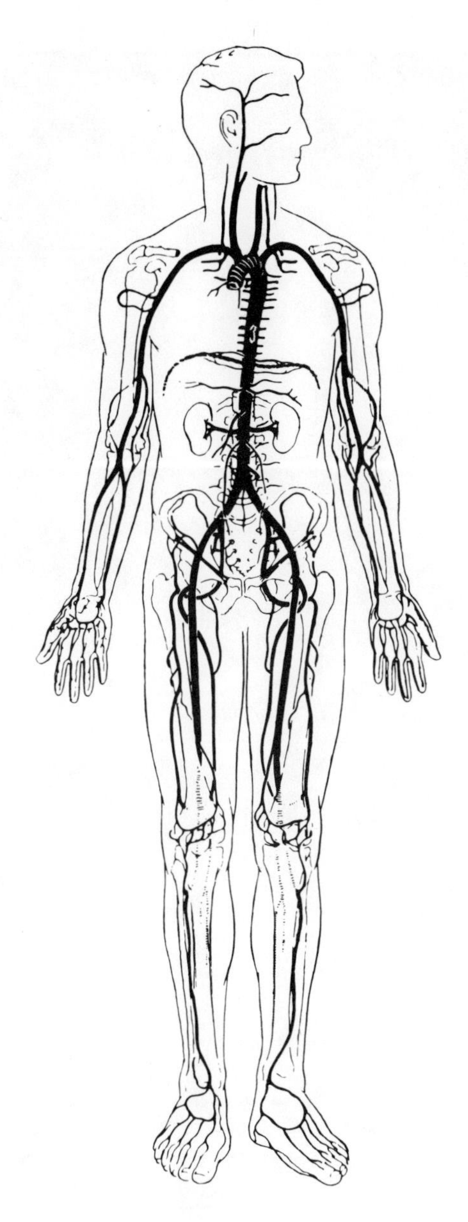

THE ARTERIAL SYSTEM.

substance. The more people smoke, the more tar builds up in their lungs and keeps them from working properly. Tar stains the lungs, but more importantly it irritates the lining of the bronchial tubes which lead to the lungs. Tar is a known *carcinogen,* which means that it can cause cancer.

CARBON MONOXIDE

Carbon monoxide is a colorless, odorless gas that is created when something doesn't burn completely. A car engine gives off carbon monoxide because it isn't 100 percent efficient and doesn't burn up all the fuel. In the same way, burning tobacco also creates carbon monoxide.

When you inhale carbon monoxide, it takes the place of the oxygen your blood would normally be carrying. This means that your heart has to work more to get enough oxygen for the body, and you have to breathe faster. Many people who smoke don't even notice that they are breathing faster to get enough oxygen, and they don't notice the extra strain this puts on their hearts.

However, some of the effects of high carbon monoxide levels in the blood can be measured. Studies have

This automatic smoking machine puffs away on cigarettes and collects the smoke residue. The tars that are trapped are used in cancer research.

shown that carbon monoxide can alter your vision and make it more difficult to tell how bright an object is. It also slows your reflexes and makes you generally slower. Mainly though, the danger of carbon monoxide is that it replaces oxygen your body needs and forces your heart to work harder than it should.

OTHER INGREDIENTS

Tobacco smoke contains dozens of other gases, liquids, and particles. Some of these are ammonia, DDT, cadmium, nitrogen oxide, carbon dioxide, formaldehyde, benzene, and hydrogen sulphide. Tobacco smoke also contains benzopyrene, which is a suspected carcinogen. Each of these ingredients taken into the body separately is unhealthy. Taken all together, which is what you do when you smoke, they are downright dangerous. The next few chapters will show you just how dangerous smoking can be.

SMOKING AND YOUR LUNGS

HOW YOUR LUNGS WORK

Every person has to breathe in oxygen in order to live. It's even more important than food and water, since you can only live a few minutes without it.

When you breathe in, the oxygen you inhale goes to your two lungs, which are located in your chest. As the oxygen enters the lungs it passes through a series of passages that get smaller and smaller. At the end of the smallest passages, there are thousands of tiny air sacs called *alveoli.* The oxygen passes through the walls of the air sacs into blood vessels where red blood cells are waiting to carry it to all parts of your body. These red blood cells then drop off the oxygen in some part of the body and pick up carbon dioxide, a waste product.

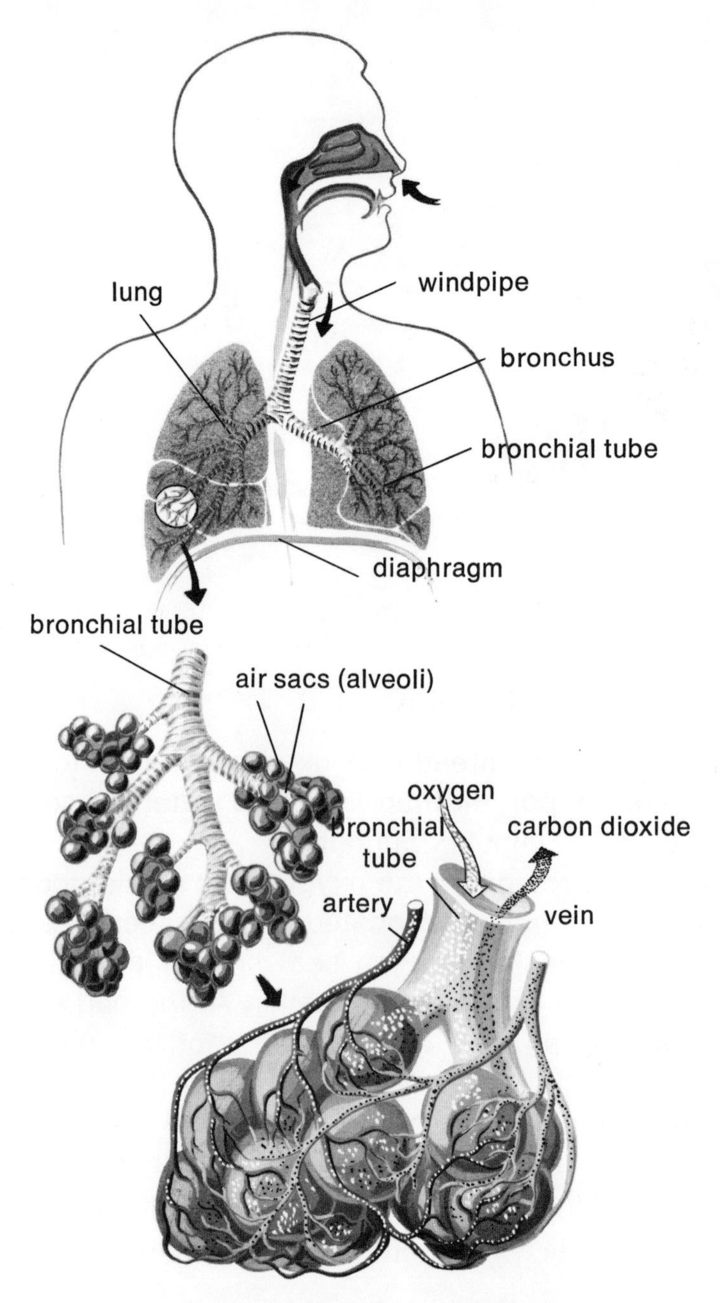

THE RESPIRATORY SYSTEM.

The blood cells carry it back to the air sacs so that the lungs can get rid of it when you breathe out, or exhale. This process of inhaling oxygen and exhaling carbon dioxide takes place every time you breathe in and out. You don't even have to think about it—your body does it automatically.

When you need more oxygen—when you exercise, play, or dance—your body automatically breathes faster so that the lungs can take in more oxygen. Your chest muscles work harder so you can breathe more deeply, and your heart pumps faster to move your blood more quickly. That's when you feel "out of breath." But when you're sleeping, resting, or just doing something quiet, you need less oxygen and you breathe more slowly and less deeply, again without thinking about it. Your lungs, working together with your heart, are extraordinary machines!

KEEPING THE MACHINE CLEAN

When you breathe, the air you inhale has more than oxygen in it. It also contains germs, dirt, and tiny particles of solid matter. Many of these are trapped in your mouth and nose before they reach the lungs. But even those that manage to get past the mouth and nose are trapped in a number of ways.

The passages to the lungs are lined with special glands that produce *mucus,* a sticky substance that catches and holds germs and dirt. This mucus is moved by tiny hairlike projections called *cilia* that constantly move back and forth like tall grass in the wind. The cilia move the mucus carrying dirt and germs up toward the mouth where it is swallowed, taken to the stomach, and safely expelled. If a very large particle of dirt or mucus gets stuck, you can blast it out with a cough or a sneeze. So Nature has not only designed a wonderful machine, but it has also provided it with its own cleaning system!

But like all machines that aren't given proper care, your lungs can break down. That's when disease, and even death, steps in and takes over.

LUNG CANCER

Lung cancer, like all other cancers, usually starts with a single cell. Just why a cell becomes cancerous is still not known, although we do know that there are some substances, such as those found in tobacco smoke, that seem to cause cancer. In any case, the single cancerous cell may multiply until it forms a lump of cancerous tissue called a tumor.

Tumors in the lungs are very difficult to see on X-rays. They are generally quite large and have already caused other symptoms, such as coughing up blood, before a doctor can spot them. This is the reason there is little success in treating lung cancer compared with other kinds of cancer. By the time doctors operate to remove the growth, the cancer has generally spread to other parts of the lungs or body. Lung cancer cells tend to spread faster than other kinds of cancer cells because the lungs have a particularly rich supply of

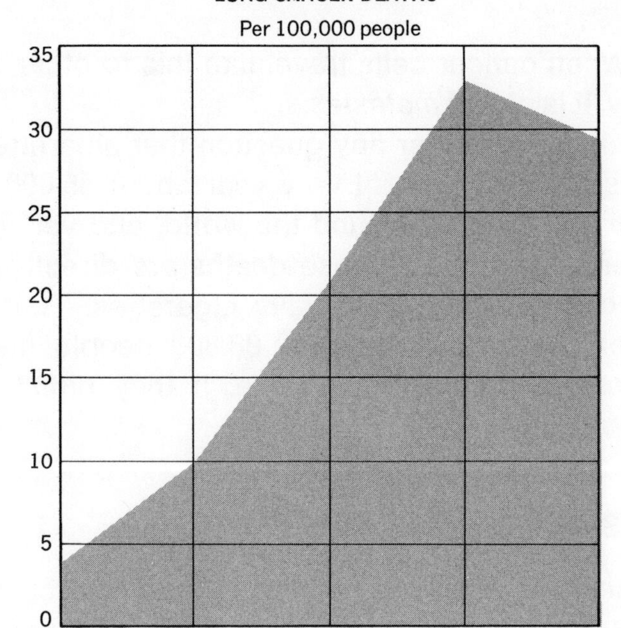
LUNG CANCER DEATHS
Per 100,000 people
35
30
25
20
15
10
5
0
1930
1940
1950
1960
1970

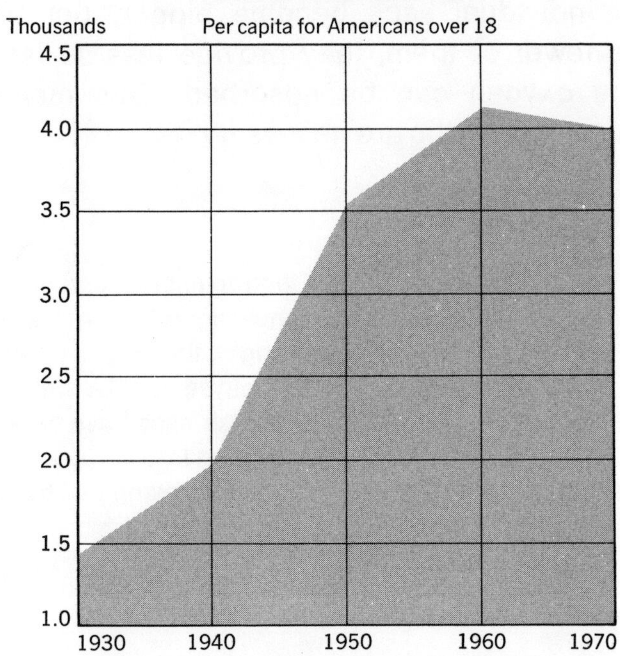
CIGARETTE CONSUMPTION
Thousands
Per capita for Americans over 18
4.5
4.0
3.5
3.0
2.5
2.0
1.5
1.0
1930
1940
1950
1960
1970

blood. When cancer cells travel like this to other parts of the body, it is called *metastasis*.

There is no longer any question that cigarette smoking causes lung cancer. Every year about 85,000 people die from this disease around the world, and yet we know that over 80 percent of those deaths are directly caused by tobacco smoking, especially cigarettes. That means that every year approximately 68,800 people die needlessly, only because they smoke. If they didn't smoke, they would stay alive.

EMPHYSEMA

Emphysema is a disease of the lungs in which the tiny air sacs that transmit oxygen to the blood are broken down and destroyed. As the walls between the sacs collapse, individual sacs become bigger, but because there are fewer of them, they provide less surface from which the oxygen can be absorbed. This means that more and more breaths are necessary.

Electron microscope photographs showing: left, a normal lung, and right, the lung of a person with emphysema. The walls between the air sacs have broken down, providing less surface from which oxygen can be absorbed.

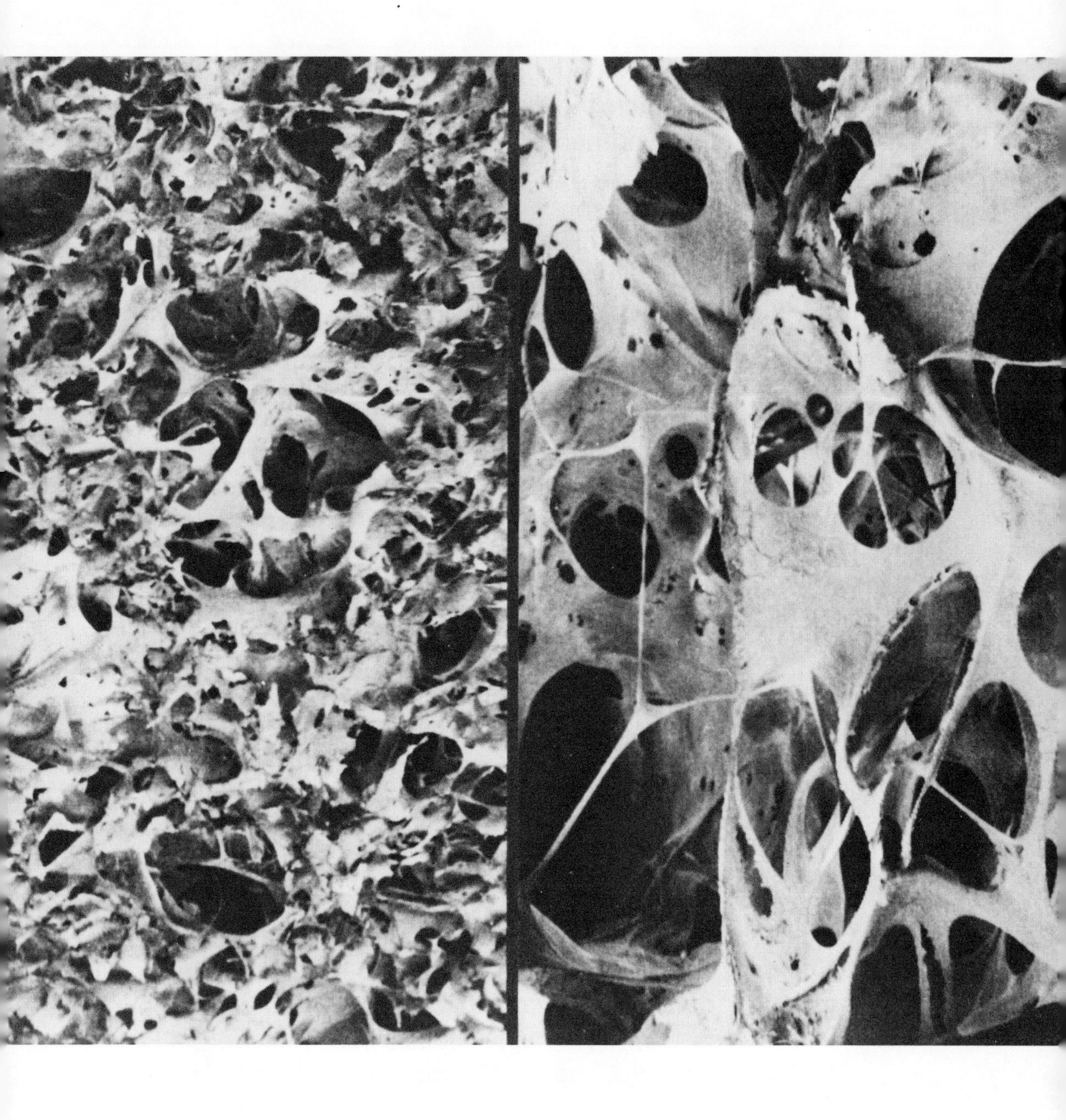

This slow breaking down of the air sacs can take years, during which the person with emphysema has to struggle harder and harder for enough oxygen. A normal adult uses about 5 percent of his or her energy for breathing, but a person with advanced emphysema may need up to 80 percent of his or her *total* energy just to breathe. Normal activity becomes impossible, and eventually the person suffocates to death.

The chances of getting emphysema are about *six times* greater for people who smoke than for people who don't smoke. While the exact cause of the disease isn't known, there are two theories. It may be that the lung's arteries become obstructed or narrowed as a reaction to smoke. This decreases the blood supply to lung tissues, which may then break down and lose their ability to work. It may also be that the many known poisonous or toxic substances in tobacco smoke attack the lung tissues directly and make them stop working. It's possible that both these theories are correct and work together. Whatever the exact process, it's certain that smoking increases your chances of getting this painful and usually fatal disease.

CHRONIC BRONCHITIS

Chronic bronchitis (CB) is a condition that results from a buildup of mucus in the lungs and its bronchial passages. CB causes a person to cough constantly, since that's the only way the excess mucus can be removed.

The longer you have CB, the worse it gets since

more and more mucus fills up the passages of the lungs and that leaves less and less space for oxygen. You have to breathe more and more to get all the oxygen you need.

There are other causes of CB besides smoking, but people who smoke are *six times* as likely to get it as non-smokers. That's because the inhaled smoke damages the cilia, those little hairlike projections, and they can no longer move mucus out of the lungs.

Studies have shown that a teenager who smokes as little as five cigarettes a day coughs as much and spits up as much mucus as an adult who smokes heavily. This is probably because the tissues of a young person's body are more sensitive and react more strongly to the harsh effects of tobacco smoke. In addition, people who have CB are more likely to get all sorts of other lung infections. Any of these infections can rob your body of the oxygen it needs.

Your body's need for oxygen is the most important need you have, more important than food and water. Your lungs are the way your body takes in that oxygen. Even if you don't develop cancer, emphysema, chronic bronchitis, or some other lung infection, smoking prevents your lungs from working as well as they can. It cuts down on your whole body's efficiency. And even if you don't know all the bad things smoking does to your body, even if you can't see the insides of your lungs and how "dirty" and clogged smoking makes them, it doesn't really matter. Your lungs, and the rest of your body, know the difference.

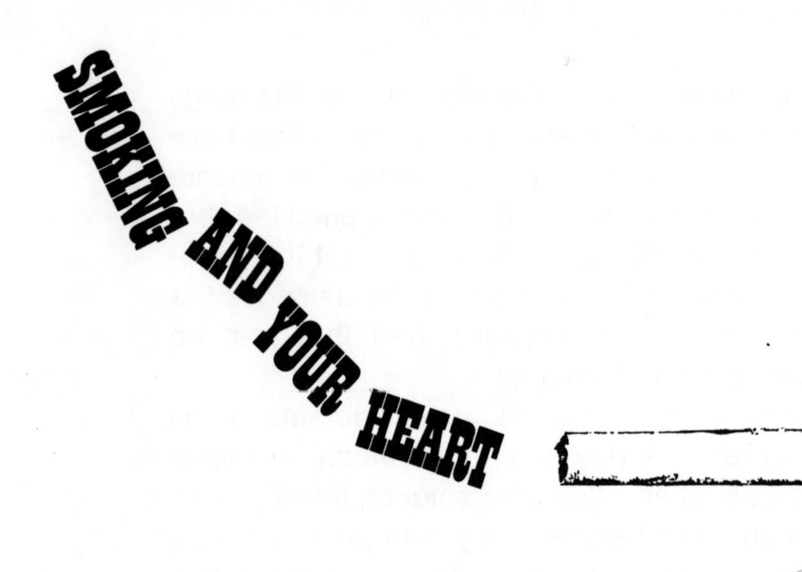

Coronary heart disease is the most frequent cause of death in the United States. This is also true in Great Britain. In addition, it is the major cause of "excess" deaths among cigarette smokers.

There are generally three factors involved in heart attacks. These are:

1. High cholesterol in the blood. Cholesterol is a fat-soluble substance that narrows arteries.

2. High blood pressure. Blood pressure is the measurement of the amount of tension in the walls of blood vessels and is determined by the rate at which blood flows through those vessels.

3. Lack of exercise, and *obesity,* which means being greatly overweight.

People who have none of these factors but who

RISK FACTORS IN HEART ATTACK AND STROKE

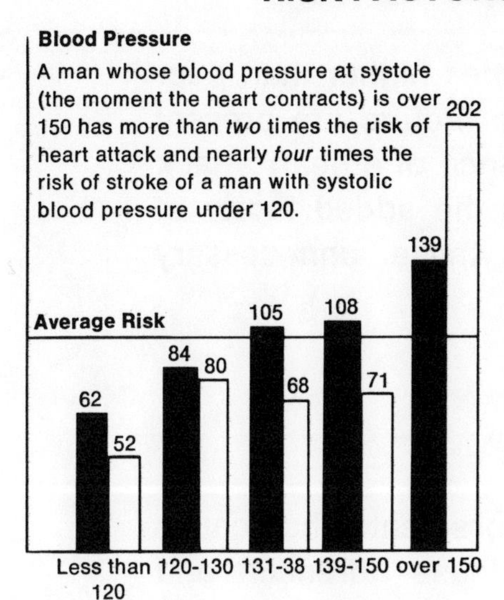

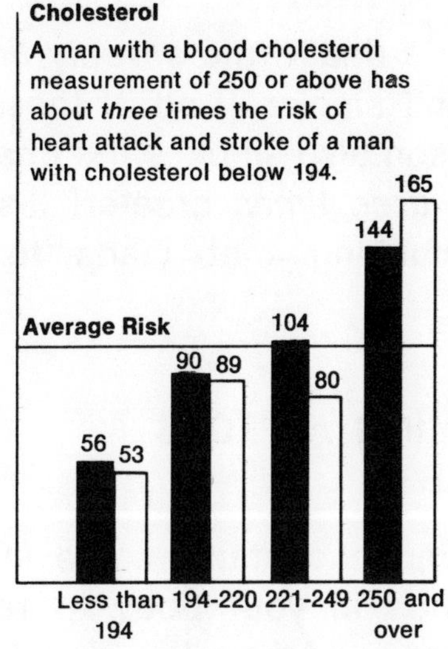

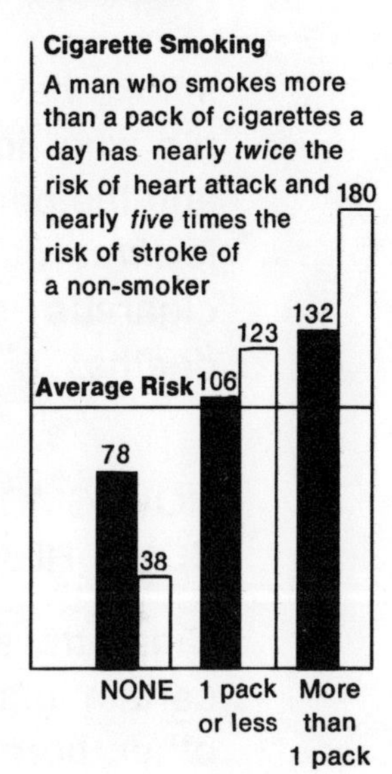

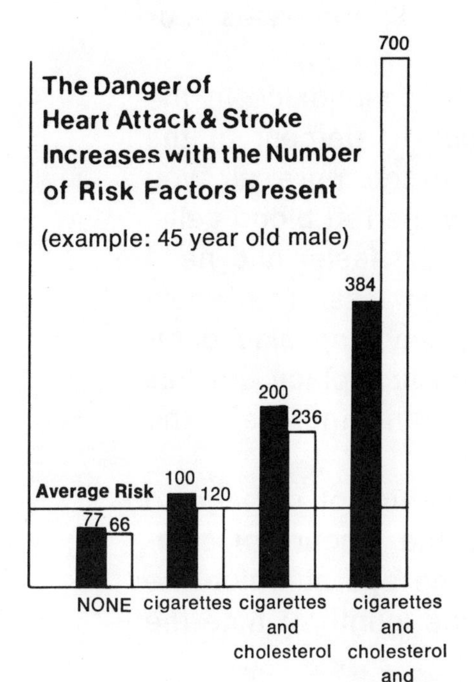

These charts show the extent to which particular risk factors increased the risk of heart attack and stroke in the male population, aged 30-62 of Framingham, Mass. For each disease, columns below the black horizontal line indicate lower than average risk; columns above the line, higher than average risk.

Heart Attack

Stroke (Atherothrombotic Brain Infarction)

This chart shows how a combination of three major risk factors can increase the likelihood of heart attack and stroke. For purposes of illustration, this chart uses an abnormal blood pressure level of 180 systolic, and a cholesterol level of 310 in a 45-year old man.

Source: The Framingham, Mass. Heart Study

smoke have a death rate *seventy times* higher than people who don't smoke. If all of these factors are present and the person also smokes the chance of a heart attack is *three hundred times* greater! It's the added factor of cigarette smoking that leads to these unnecessary deaths.

HOW SMOKING AFFECTS YOUR HEART

Cigarette smoke contains some ingredients that cause certain glands in your body to release adrenalin and other hormones. Adrenalin is a hormone that speeds up your heart. It causes the walls of the heart to contract more strongly and more often, and it increases your heart's need for oxygen.

But at the same time, the carbon monoxide in the smoke drives out or replaces about 10 percent of the oxygen that would ordinarily be in the pure air you breathe and that would be carried by the red blood cells. So while smoking makes the heart beat faster and need more oxygen, it also causes it to get less. The whole process is made even worse since smoking also damages the lungs that take in air in the first place. All this puts a greater strain on your heart and increases the chances of having a heart attack.

Studies have shown that the amount of damage to the heart is in direct proportion to the amount of cigarettes a person smokes each day, the age at which the person first begins to smoke, and the length of time the

Your Heart and How it Works

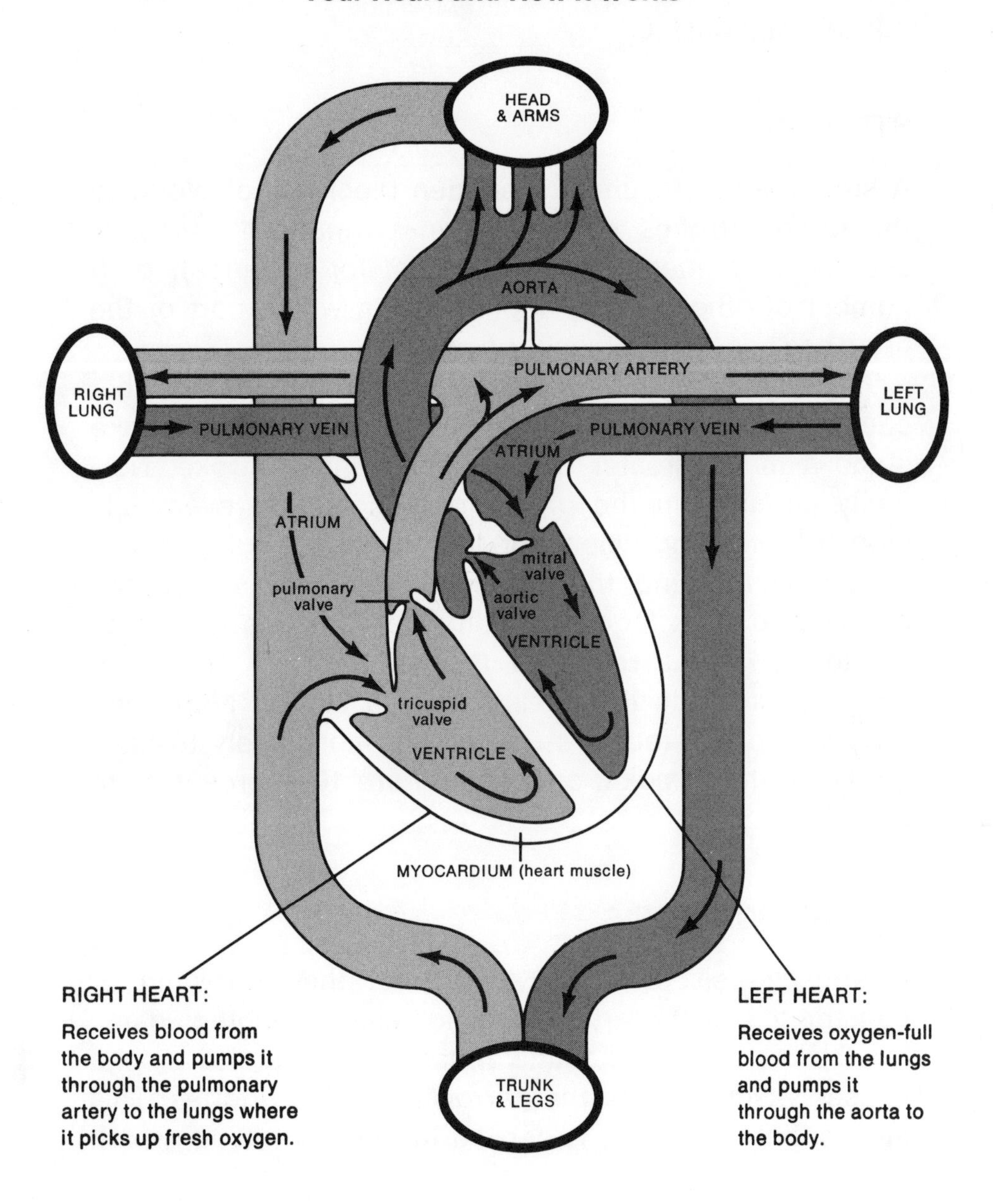

person has been a smoker. This is what doctors call a "dose" relationship.

STROKES

A stroke is the result of a sudden blockage of blood to the brain. Strokes can result in permanent paralysis, speech impairment (slurring words, for instance), or a number of other things, depending on which part of the brain has been without enough oxygen.

Generally it is the presence of a blood clot that causes the blockage to the brain. People who smoke stand a much greater chance of having a stroke. Normally platelets in the blood form clots that eventually stop the bleeding when, for instance, you cut yourself. It has been found that smoking seems to cause the platelets to stick together even when there is no bleeding to stop. As a result, clots float through the bloodstream increasing the likelihood of a stroke. Men aged forty-five to fifty-four are 50 percent more likely to have strokes if they smoke, and women are 100 percent more likely!

ARTERIOSCLEROSIS

Arteriosclerosis is a fancy word for the narrowing or constricting of the arteries. Vasoplasm is another name for this condition. Nicotine inhaled in cigarette smoke causes vasoplasm, or the narrowing of the arteries. This means that less blood is carried to the heart itself, which

CAUSE OF DEATH AMONG CIGARETTE SMOKERS.

Underlying cause of death	**Expected deaths**[1]	**Recorded deaths**[2]	**Mortality ratio**[3]
Cancer of lung	170.3	1,833	10.8
Bronchitis and emphysema	89.5	546	6.1
Cancer of larynx	14.0	75	5.4
Other circulatory diseases	254.0	649	2.6
Cirrhosis of liver	169.2	379	2.2
Coronary artery disease	6,430.7	11,177	1.7
Other heart diseases	526.0	868	1.7
Hypertensive heart	409.2	631	1.5
General arteriosclerosis	210.7	310	1.5
All causes	15,653.9	23,223	1.68

(1) Expected deaths: Figure given shows the number of deaths considered normal among non-smokers.

(2) Recorded deaths: Figure given shows actual deaths recorded among the smokers in the study.

(3) Mortality ratio: Ratio of 2 means that death rate is twice as high for smokers as for non-smokers.

(Source: Adapted from U.S. Department of Health, Education and Welfare, Smoking and Health.)

results in damaged heart tissue. It also means that because less blood can pass through the narrowed arteries, the heart has to work overtime under a greater strain.

In addition, the arteries of people who smoke have been found to contain a greater number of fatty plaques, or tiny pieces of fatty tissue. These stick to the walls of the arteries and make them even more narrow, allowing less blood to pass through them. All of this adds to the chance of having a heart attack or other diseases that have to do with the heart and blood system.

Even if you're lucky enough not to suffer from any of these diseases of the heart, the fact is that smoking puts an unnecessary strain on your heart. Smoking also makes your lungs less efficient and makes it harder to breathe normally. Smoking makes it harder to be active —to play football or swim or dance or whatever you like to do. It makes it harder to have fun—it makes it harder to be you!

OTHER DANGERS OF SMOKING

MORE CANCER

There are other sorts of cancers that seem to be related to smoking besides lung cancer. People who smoke run the risk of getting cancers in all the places the smoke they breathe in touches. For instance, all smokers are *four times* as likely to develop cancer of the mouth (which includes the lips, tongue, hard palate, etc.) than people who don't smoke.

The figures are even higher for cancer of the larynx, which is where the vocal cords are located. Cigarette smokers are *three to eighteen times* more likely to get this kind of cancer than nonsmokers; for pipe and cigar smokers the chances are *seven to ten times* greater.

Another kind of cancer smokers develop more frequently is cancer of the esophagus, the pipe that goes down to your stomach. Smokers are *two to six times* as likely to get cancer of the esophagus than people who don't smoke.

ORGAN CANCERS

It's easy to forget that it isn't just the smoke itself that's harmful to your body, it's all the poisonous compounds and other ingredients that the smoke contains. All these dangerous things are passed from the smoke you breathe into your blood by the lungs. This means that all the organs of a smoker's body are in greater danger of developing cancer than those of a nonsmoker. This is especially true of those organs whose job is to cleanse the blood and get rid of the wastes your body produces.

Studies have shown that smokers develop cancer of the urinary bladder *seven to ten times* more often than nonsmokers. They are also *twice* as likely to get cancer of the kidneys. In addition, the urine of smokers has been found to contain a chemical known to cause bladder cancer, even if the smoker hasn't yet developed the cancer.

The most important thing to remember is that the wonderful way the lungs transfer the air you breathe into oxygen for the blood also means that the impurities you inhale in that air, and especially all the harmful things in tobacco smoke, also get transferred to your blood. And your blood travels to every part of your body. The "cleaner" your blood is, the less chance of things going wrong with your body.

WOMEN AND SMOKING

Until recently, people thought that for some reason women were less likely to develop lung cancer than men. The facts showed that a smaller proportion of women got the disease than men. But in the last few years the percentage of women smokers who get lung cancer has greatly increased. The reason for this is simple: more women smoke now and have smoked longer than ever before in history. Right now the lung cancer death rate for women is one-fourth the rate for men. But only a few years ago it was one-sixth. That means that each year we can expect the female death rate from lung cancer to continue to catch up to the male's—as long as more women continue to smoke.

SMOKING AND PREGNANCY

When a woman is pregnant, it is her blood that nourishes the fetus, or developing baby. If she smokes and her blood is full of impurities and carbon monoxide, these will be passed on to her unborn child. The nicotine that restricts her blood vessels will do the same to the blood vessels of the fetus. This reduces the amount of blood the baby gets. Carbon monoxide, by reducing oxygen levels, hinders normal growth in the baby.

One study showed that the babies of women who smoked weighed an average of six ounces less than babies whose mothers didn't smoke. This is especially meaningful because low birth weight is thought to be connected to higher death rates in infants and slower development in babies.

SECONDHAND SMOKING

One of the most surprising things about tobacco smoke is that the smoke a burning cigarette gives off into the air has larger quantities of dangerous ingredients than the smoke that gets inhaled by a smoker. In some studies, the smoke that goes into the air, called sidestream smoke, has been shown to be *twice* as filled with harmful chemicals as the smoke that gets directly inhaled, called mainstream smoke.

This means that if you're sitting in a room with a smoker, you're inhaling all the dangerous things the smoker is—whether you want to or not. This is definitely one reason to encourage people not to smoke when you're around—*their* smoking is dangerous to *your* health!

This fact has been measured in a number of ways. Some studies have measured the carbon monoxide content in a nonsmoker's blood after he or she has sat in a room in which other people have been smoking. After a short time, the levels of carbon monoxide in the nonsmoker's blood have gone up, and produced the same effects carbon monoxide has on smokers.

Non-smokers inhale all the dangerous things smokers inhale, and some studies have shown they are inhaling them in greater quantities.

Other studies have shown that children who grow up in homes in which the parents smoke get more colds, coughs, and respiratory infections than children who grow up in homes where neither parent smokes.

The unexpected finding that tobacco smoke affects even those people who don't smoke themselves has given rise to new laws that make it illegal to smoke in certain places, especially in small, enclosed areas like elevators. It has also produced voluntary plans to separate smokers and nonsmokers in such public places as aircraft and restaurants, not just for comfort but also for reasons of health.

Knowing that cigarette smoke can hurt the nonsmoker as well as the smoker makes it easier and much more sensible for you to say "yes" when somebody asks if you mind very much if he or she smokes.

FIRE

There's an old saying, "Where there's smoke, there's fire." That is one of the things people often forget when talking about the dangers of smoking. Cigarettes, pipes, cigars—all of them *burn.* Not only that, it takes a flame, whether from matches or lighters or something else, to light the tobacco in the first place. The sad fact is that people are often careless about matches or burning tobacco. In 1970 the U.S. National Fire Protection Association linked 107,200 building fires, with an estimated total property damage of $95.9 million, to matches and cigarettes.

MAKING UP YOUR OWN MIND

It used to be that people thought smoking was the "in" thing to do. Lots of glamorous ads and commercials (which are now prohibited by law on television) made it seem that smoking, especially cigarette smoking, was grown-up. They made the smoker appear to be a more attractive person who could do just about anything better. But that was before there was solid proof that smoking is dangerous to a person's health, and that it may even kill. Now we know that smoking even a pipe or cigar is unhealthy.

It's estimated that in the last few years thirty million people have quit smoking around the world and that millions of other people want to. It's also a fact that the majority of people don't smoke. All these people have quit or never started smoking because they know what smoking does and can do to them.

"Give up smoking? Why?"

WHAT ABOUT YOU?

When you see friends and maybe your parents smoking, it's hard to resist taking a puff to see what it's all about. It's also possible you have some friends who will tease you if you don't try smoking. But it's up to you, and you alone, whether you take that first puff—and before you do, think about it. Remember, even a few cigarettes make your body less efficient and make it harder to be good at what you like to do, whether it's sports or dancing or simply having your kind of fun.

If you've already tried smoking and don't think it's so bad, maybe you should think again. Do you really want to risk getting all the diseases smoking can cause? Do you really want to risk the worst thing of all—dying early, before your natural time? Those are hard questions to think about, but no one can answer them for you. The decision to smoke is *your* decision; you've got to make up your own mind.

WHAT ABOUT OTHERS?

If your parents or other people you love smoke, no one can force them to stop. They have to want to themselves. But you can help them along. For instance, you can tell them in a nice, matter-of-fact way that you don't like to be around them when they smoke because it hurts you to see them hurting themselves. Also you might point out that their smoke is bad for you. Your comments may be just the push they need to think seriously about quitting.

TEAM #
1
2
3
4
5
PRESENT
NON-SMOKERS
% NON-SMOKERS
# CIGARETTES SMOKED
DALLASTOWN AREA HIGH SCHOOL
SMOKING WITHDRAWAL CLINIC

Of course, it's important not to sound angry or bossy or superior when you give advice to anyone. Sometimes advice works and sometimes it doesn't, but you may want to think about making the effort—and you can always try again.

You can also look for groups in your town or city that care about the dangers of smoking and are trying to do something about it. If you're interested, you can find out what sort of laws these groups would like to see passed—laws that would control how cigarettes are advertised, what kind of cigarettes can be sold (those with low tar and nicotine are best if people have to smoke at all), and where people can and can't smoke in public places.

If you simply want more information about smoking and health, you can contact your local cancer society, lung association, or heart association. Most people who smoke would like to stop, and if you share the facts with them, it may help them finally make up their minds.

When you think about smoking and health, it's impossible not to think of all the terrible diseases your body can develop. It can get more than a little scary.

It isn't easy to stop smoking. Sometimes doing it with others helps. These high school students are part of a smoking withdrawal clinic at their school.

But one thing to keep in mind is the extraordinary fact that most of us are healthy most of the time. When your body is working normally, it's wonderfully strong!

Every day you meet up with germs, irritants, and things that can cause infections and illness. And every day your body is able to fight them off. All of us have built-in "defenders" and "cleaning systems" that are always working to keep us fit and well. Of course, there are times when things go wrong and we do get sick. But for most of us, those times don't come very often.

The fact is your body is designed to stay healthy. But it makes sense to give it all the help you can. That's why it's important to get plenty of exercise, eat good, nutritious food, and get enough rest. And it's just as important to *not* do things that can hurt your body and keep you from being the best you can be.

All the evidence shows that smoking is one of the things that hurts your body. But whether you smoke or not will be your own decision. So think hard about the facts before you make up your mind!

There is a growing concern with
the rights of non-smokers.
The waiter in an ice cream parlor
points out the "No Smoking" signs.

(59)

INDEX

ABOUT THE AUTHOR

A free-lance writer, Sherry Sonnett has written on a wide range of topics for many major periodicals. At present she is working on a biography of Emma Goldman. Smoking *is her first book for Franklin Watts, Inc. Ms. Sonnett lives in Los Angeles, California.*